Witness to History

Victorian Britain

Sean Connolly

www.heinemann.co.uk/library

Visit our website to find out more information about **Heinemann Library** books.

To order:

 Phone 44 (0) 1865 888066

 Send a fax to 44 (0) 1865 314091

 Visit the Heinemann Bookshop at www.heinemann.co.uk/library to browse our catalogue and order online.

First published in Great Britain by Heinemann Library, Halley Court, Jordan Hill, Oxford OX2 8EJ, part of Harcourt Education.

Heinemann is a registered trademark of Harcourt Education Ltd.

© Harcourt Education Ltd 2003
First published in paperback in 2004
The moral right of the proprietor has been asserted.

Produced for Heinemann by Discovery Books Ltd
Editorial: Sarah Eason and Gill Humphrey
Design: Ian Winton
Picture Research: Rachel Tisdale
Production: Edward Moore

Originated by Ambassador Litho Ltd
Printed and bound in Hong Kong, China
by South China Printing

ISBN 0 431 17045 2 (hardback)
07 06 05 04 03
10 9 8 7 6 5 4 3 2 1

ISBN 0 431 17051 7 (paperback)
08 07 06 05 04
10 9 8 7 6 5 4 3 2 1

British Library Cataloguing in Publication Data
Connolly, Sean
  Victorian Britain. – (Witness to History)
  941'.081
A full catalogue record for this book is available from the British Library.

Acknowledgements
The publishers would like to thank the following for permission to reproduce photographs:
Bettmann/Hulton p.**16**; The Fleming–Wyfold Art Foundation/Bridgeman Art Library p.**33**; Hermitage, St Petersburg/Bridgeman Art Library p.**45**; Corbis p.**21**; Mary Evans Picture Library pp.**4, 5, 6, 7, 10, 14, 17, 18, 19, 20, 24, 25, 26, 32, 36, 40, 41, 42, 43, 44, 45, 48, 50**; Hulton Archive pp.**34, 46**; Hulton Getty p.**35**; Mansell/Timepix/Rex Features pp.**28, 38**; Peter Newark's Historical Pictures pp.**8, 12, 22, 30**; Robert Opie Collection p.**27**.

Cover photograph is an 1898 illustration showing a 'crossing-sweeper' boy being paid by a wealthy Victorian lady for sweeping her pathway on the road. This picture is reproduced with permission of Mary Evans Picture Library.

The publishers would like to thank Bob Rees, historian and assistant head teacher, for his assistance in the preparation of this book.

Disclaimer
All Internet addresses (URLs) given in this book were valid at the time of going to press. However, due to the dynamic nature of the Internet, some addresses may have changed, or sites may have changed or ceased to exist since publication. While the author and publisher regret any inconvenience this may cause readers, no responsibility for any such changes can be accepted by either the author or the publisher.

Every effort has been made to contact copyright holders of any material reproduced in this book. Any omissions will be rectified in subsequent printings if notice is given to the publishers.

Words appearing in bold, **like this,** are explained in the Glossary.

Contents

Introduction

The Victorian era (1837–1901) was a time of rapid change, economic growth and, for some, great prosperity. At the start of Queen Victoria's reign Britain was mainly an agricultural nation, but by the time of her death more than three-quarters of the population lived in towns or cities. New inventions and faster machines developed as a result of the **Industrial Revolution** fuelled the growth of industrial cities. A few people benefited, becoming very rich, as new factories were built and **manufacturing** and trade flourished. For the vast majority of working people, however, earning a few pennies each day and keeping out of the **workhouse** were their main concerns.

The British Empire

From the seventeenth century onwards Britain had begun to gain control of many other parts of the world. Most of these lands became British **colonies**, where local officials made some decisions, but overall power was still based in London. By the time Victoria became queen, Great Britain controlled Australia, New Zealand and Canada, as well as some parts of Africa, the Caribbean and Asia. During Victoria's reign, this process of colonization continued. British influence, driven by business, military power and a desire to spread the Christian gospel, took root in the colonies. British officials governed many of these areas like smaller versions of Britain itself, with British-style law courts, schools and rail networks. One of the most memorable events of the century came in 1877, when Victoria was crowned Empress of India. The British-controlled lands spread around the world were no longer simply a collection of colonies – they had become the British Empire.

This is one of the most famous photographs of Queen Victoria. It was taken in 1887, ten years after she was crowned Empress of India.

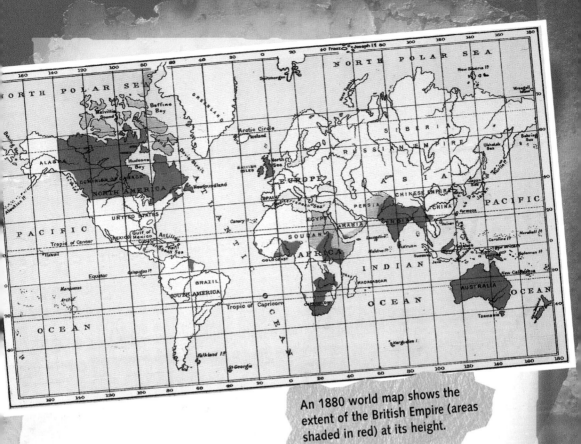

An 1880 world map shows the extent of the British Empire (areas shaded in red) at its height.

Ideas of progress

Many Victorians were concerned with the idea of progress and during this era Great Britain became the most powerful nation on earth. Some Victorians believed that progress would also be good for the rest of the world. For them, having an empire was not only a way of getting cheap goods from around the world, it was a chance to spread British ideas and achievements to other countries.

However, not all Victorians approved of change. People working in towns and in the countryside saw machines taking over traditional jobs. Many looked back fondly to a time when landscapes were not ruined by the sight of factory chimneys billowing black smoke. Others saw their houses and common land cleared away to make way for larger, more efficient farms. Unfortunately it was often the poor who made the biggest sacrifices in the name of progress.

How do we know?

By studying history, we can learn about the events of the past. If we need to find out about, for example, the origin of the Olympic Games in Greece or the French Revolution, we can find many books and articles about these subjects. They can tell us when and how these events took place, as well as who were the leading characters. They often go on to explain not only why things have happened, by giving the background to the events, but also how the events themselves changed the course of history. A historical work that is written after the period it describes is called a **secondary source**.

Getting to the source

This book uses **primary sources** to tell the story of life in Victorian Britain. Secondary sources can give us the broad picture of events and changes in this historical period, but primary sources capture the 'feel'

of the times, highlighting the fast-moving changes that amazed some people and horrified others. These sources, which include diary entries, newspaper reports, **memoirs** and advertisements, put real people back into the historical picture with personal accounts that describe what it was really like to be alive during the reign of Queen Victoria.

For most people letter writing was the only way of communicating before the introduction of the telephone. Nineteenth-century letters give us first-hand accounts of how Victorian people lived and felt.

Photography was developed during the Victorian era, providing us with accurate pictures of lfe at that time, such as this image of Coventry factory workers in 1897.

A varied picture

The Victorian era was a time of new ideas. As happens with many new ideas, people often resisted them at first. You can sense in his writing Charles Darwin's concern about the public response to his great work *On the Origin of Species* (see page 17). Other documents served to alert the public to dangers or to make political points. Annie Besant's description of the working conditions in the match factories (see page 37) and James Greenwood's account of the **temperance** meeting (see page 31) are good examples. However, those who lived away from such problems often found it easy to ignore the cruelty and injustices that flourished throughout Victorian society.

Many of the other accounts are simply descriptions of developments in a fast-changing world. Together these accounts paint a vivid picture of life in this fascinating period of British history.

Forging new links

At the time of Queen Victoria's coronation in 1837, Great Britain was changing fast. Scientists, engineers and company owners were taking advantage of the new technology created by the **Industrial Revolution**. New techniques in mining, farming and **manufacturing** enabled people to produce more goods. These goods were then sold in Great Britain and also shipped and sold to people in other countries around the world.

The Industrial Revolution was dependent on the development of a good transport system. People could no longer rely on horse-drawn vehicles to carry loads, often on rutted, muddy roads. Factory owners needed a regular supply of coal to operate their steam-powered machines and, like farmers, then had to send their goods to towns and cities where people would buy them. Looking for new ways to carry heavy loads, engineers in the eighteenth century had begun developing a network of canals to transport goods in large, flat-bottomed boats. New paving methods, pioneered by engineers such as John McAdam, made road travel quicker and safer. In the 1820s Britain saw the introduction of a new form of transport – the railway. The new steam trains moved goods much faster than canal boats, and by the late 1820s had even begun attracting passengers. During the Victorian era over 32,000 kilometres (20,000 miles) of track would be laid. Journeys that once lasted days now took only hours.

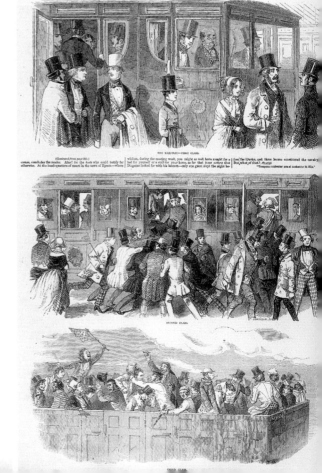

The Aylesbury News

15 June 1839

Monday last was indeed a gay and busy day. At an early hour inhabitants of this town were aroused by the lively strains of the Aylesbury town band, and great numbers of people were present to witness the departure of the seven o'clock (first) train. At ten o'clock the crowd of respectable inhabitants and fashionably dressed people around the station-house was very great, and the pressure to obtain the best seats was severe. None were admitted without a shareholder's ticket, and as soon as the train was full the band struck up and off went the steamer, dragging after it [in the carriages] between 200 and 300 people, and to the amazement of as many thousands outside, who were regretting their ill-luck in not having obtained a ticket. The train returned from Cheddington almost immediately, and from that time till night, the crowd, besieged the station house clamouring for admission.

This humorous illustration from 1847 shows the different conditions for rail passengers in first class (top), second class and third class (bottom).

The Penny Post

British people had been able to post letters before the 1800s, but the service was costly and unreliable. Worse still, the person receiving the letter – and not the sender – had to pay for the delivery. Letter carriers sometimes had to make five or six calls at a house before someone would receive, and pay for, the letter. Then in the mid-1830s a teacher named Rowland Hill made a new suggestion. He said that mail could be delivered more efficiently, and more cheaply, if the sender paid with a stamp. He suggested a flat rate of one penny for each ounce (30g.) a letter weighed. This was far less than the sixpence people had been paying. Hill made his proposal to the government in 1837 and Parliament eventually approved his suggestion in 1839.

The Uniform Penny Post came into force on 10 January 1840. On the first day of the Penny Post 112,000 letters were posted, more than three times the number for that day in the previous year. In 1840, after the introduction of the Penny Post, 168 million letters were posted in Great Britain. Ten years later this figure had risen to 347 million letters.

The Penny Post arrived at a time when many British people could not read or write. Once the educational developments of later decades took effect, the numbers of letters posted skyrocketed.

True or false?
This account describes an incident that may have inspired Rowland Hill to propose the idea of the Penny Post. We can only think of this source as a story, as we do not know if it is true or false. This account does show how the cost of receiving a letter was too much for poor people to pay, and how a more efficient and fairer way of paying for delivery would help people.

By chance he [Hill] witnessed a touching scene, a postman brought a letter from London addressed to a young village girl. She examined the letter, but because the postage on it was so great she refused to accept it. Rowland Hill intervened but the girl was clearly embarrassed by his action. Patiently he questioned her and she finally confessed that the letter was from her fiance working in London, but as she was too poor to afford letters from him they had devised a neat strategem. By various ingenious signs and marks drawn on the covering of the letter the young man was able to let her know that he was keeping well and that he still loved her.

Rowland was profoundly disturbed by this story and he pondered on the problem.

London's first post office letterbox was installed in 1855. Signs gave a clear idea of how far it was from the central post office and when letters would be collected from it.

Public health

For most people, living conditions in London and other major industrial cities were very bad in the first decades of Victoria's reign. Poor **hygiene**, open drains (underground sewers were not built until the 1860s), overcrowded housing, dangerous working conditions and dirty drinking water were a major part of the problem. Added to this were London's famous 'pea-soupers' – days of dense, blinding smog caused by burning coal.

All of these unhealthy factors led to outbreaks of serious illnesses, which spread quickly through the crowded city streets. Most of the victims of these diseases were poor, working people. Thousands died in the **cholera epidemics** of 1831, 1848, 1853 and 1866. **Tuberculosis** also claimed lives because the medical advances needed to cure it had not yet been made.

Edwin Chadwick (author of a public health report in 1842 – *The Sanitary Condition of the Labouring Population*) – argued that it was very difficult for poor people to improve their own living and working conditions. The first Public Health **Act** of 1848, tried to improve sanitation and building standards, but it wasn't until the 1875 Public Health Act became law, and councils were forced to provide lighting, clean water, drainage, sewage disposal and medical inspectors, that dramatic improvements in public health were made.

The French artist Gustave Doré depicted the dismal and unhealthy living conditions of working people in Whitechapel (East London) in 1872.

A gentleman, named Knight, rashly, and in ignorance of the locality, purchased the lease of No. 1, which forms the eastern end of Bethnal-Green-road. Immediately after taking up his residence there he became ill, and, shortly after, died of **typhus**, in an aggravated form. On inspection of the neighbouring premises, I discovered Paradise Dairy immediately behind his house. In this dairy sixteen cows and twenty swine are usually kept. The animal remains and decomposing vegetable refuse were piled up a considerable height above a hollow adapted to receive them. This conservation [keeping] of the refuse takes place in order that a sufficiently large quantity may accumulate. Moreover, the soakage from the neighbouring privies [toilets] found its way into this receptacle for manure and filth. The surface of the yard was dirty and covered with refuse. Even in the street, the offensiveness of this nuisance was obviously apparent to every passer-by. The occupiers of this dairy nevertheless claimed the place to be perfectly clean and wholesome.

The long arm of the law

Many of the same conditions that contributed to the poor state of public health also led to a serious crime problem in Victorian Britain. Once again the worst affected areas were London and the major cities. Poverty played a large part in leading some people into a life of crime. Violent attacks and robberies, murder and burglary were common problems in these cities. And with no streetlights in the first decades of Victoria's reign, many law-abiding people were afraid to go out at night. Newspaper reports only added to the public's fears over crime by recounting gruesome tales of murders, including those committed by the notorious Jack the Ripper in London during the late 1880s.

Britain's first police force, had been established in London in 1829. Policemen were called 'Bobbies' after their founder, Sir Robert Peel. These policemen, and similar forces in other cities, set out to make the streets safer. For those criminals who were caught and convicted, the punishments were as fierce as the crimes. Until 1846, many of them were **transported** to Australia or other British **colonies**. For others, the sentence was more clear-cut – death by hanging.

Mounted officers in London and other British cities were part of a growing police force trained to bring criminals to justice. This picture is dated 1867.

I was a witness of the execution at Horsemonger Lane this morning. I went there with the intention of observing the crowd gathered to behold it, and I had excellent opportunities of doing so, at intervals all through the night, and continuously from day-break until after the spectacle was over ...The horrors of the **gibbet** and of the crime which brought the wretched murderers to it faded in my mind before the atrocious bearing, looks, and language of the assembled spectators. When I came upon the scene at midnight, the shrillness of the cries and howls that were raised from time to time ... made my blood run cold ...When the day dawned, thieves, low prostitutes, ruffians, and vagabonds of every kind, flocked on to the ground, with every variety of offensive and foul behaviour ...When the two miserable creatures who attracted all this ghastly sight about them were turned quivering into the air, there was no more emotion, no more pity, no more thought that two immortal souls had gone to judgement, no more restraint in any of the previous obscenities, than if the name of Christ had never been heard in this world, and there were no belief among men but that they perished like the beasts.

Science and invention

Scientists, engineers and inventors were seen as important people in Vicorian times. The engineer Isambard Kingdom Brunel built railway lines, bridges and tunnels, steamships and huge new railway stations. British scientists like Michael Faraday conducted numerous tests before coming up with new theories. Faraday's work on electricity took place over 40 years, but his discoveries led to the development of the electric motor, the dynamo and the transformer. A major advance in medicine, made by Joseph Lister, was the use of **antiseptics** in the operating theatre.

Later in the era some of these discoveries were put to practical use. Electricity was used, first to send messages by telegraph and then, at the end of the nineteenth century, to provide lighting in streets and in homes. Engineers and inventors also developed the modern flush toilet, the safety pin, the rubber tyre, the bicycle and the steam **turbine**.

One of the most important scientific advances of the nineteenth century was the theory of **evolution**, developed by the English **naturalist** Charles Darwin. In his book *On the Origin of Species by Means of Natural Selection* (1859), Darwin concluded that all living creatures change over time, with the strongest or most adaptable being most likely to survive and reproduce. His theory caused an outcry by suggesting that human beings evolved from apes. This was shocking to many Christian Victorians who believed in the biblical story, which said that humans had been created by God.

Isambard Kingdom Brunel, the great Victorian engineer, stands in front of his steamship *Great Eastern*, which was launched in 1858.

At the end of his book *On the Origin of Species*, Darwin, no doubt aware of the controversy it was likely to cause among some Victorian Christians, was careful to include God in his view of the world.

It is interesting to contemplate a tangled bank, clothed with many plants of different kinds, with birds singing on the bushes, with various insects flitting about, and with worms crawling through the damp earth, and to reflect that these elaborately constructed forms, so different from each other, and dependent upon each other in so complex a manner, have all been produced by laws acting around us ... there is grandeur in this view of life, with its several powers, having been originally breathed by the Creator into a few forms or into one; and that, whilst this planet has gone cycling on according to the fixed law of gravity, from so simple a beginning endless forms most beautiful and most wonderful have been, and are being evolved.

Many Victorians mocked Darwin's theory that humans evolved from apes. This magazine illustration from the *London Sketch Book* of 1874 has Darwin trying to show an ape how similar they are.

The Great Exhibition

Inspired by a sense of pride in Britain's achievements – but with an eye on making a profit – a group of Victorians, led by Queen Victoria's husband, Prince Albert, decided to stage a Great Exhibition in London. Albert acted as president of the **Royal Commission**, which planned and later developed the exhibition.

The Great Exhibition was meant to demonstrate British achievement in industrial design while at the same time advertising British products for overseas customers. The exhibition was held in an iron-and-glass structure, known as the Crystal Palace, in London's Hyde Park. The building was enormous, covering an area of 7.5 hectares. Open for five and a half months in the summer of 1851, it attracted more than 6 million visitors, who came to see some 14,000 exhibits from around the world, nearly half of which were British. The displays ranged from examples of decorative arts to scientific instruments, tools and kitchen appliances. A large area was given over to machinery, some of it powered by the Exhibition's own steam engines.

The Exhibition was a great success, and made a huge profit. This money went towards the founding of the Victoria and Albert Museum, the Natural History Museum and the Science Museum in South Kensington, London. The Crystal Palace was taken down and re-erected in South London, but was destroyed by fire in 1936.

Victoria's husband, Prince Albert, played an important role in the planning of the Great Exhibition. He believed that such a collection of works of art and industry would encourage competition. Albert died in 1861 and was mourned by Queen Victoria for the rest of her life.

A souvenir card of the Great Exhibition gives an idea of the grand scale of the Crystal Palace in London's Hyde Park.

Responses to the Great Exhibition

The *Art Journal*, in its catalogue of the Exhibition (top), gives a dramatic description of the inside of the Crystal Palace. The quote from the *(Roman) Sun* describes the effect of the Great Exhibition on the surrounding district (bottom).

On entering the building for the first time, the eye is completely dazzled by the rich variety of hues [colours] that burst upon it on every side ... in the centre of the building rises the gigantic fountain ... whilst at the northern end the eye is relieved by the verdure [lushness] of the tropical plants and the lofty and overshadowing branches of the forest ... the first objects which attract the eye are the sculptures...

The *Art Journal 1851*

The roads leading to Hyde Park were rendered almost impassable ... It is scarcely necessary to mention that signs of a general holiday were everywhere shown, by the closing of shops and the hanging out of flags, of all nations, from the windows.

The *(Roman) Sun* 1 May 1851

Child labour

Behind Britain's prosperity in the nineteenth century lay a shameful record of harsh working conditions, especially for children. The many new factories that had developed since the beginning of the **Industrial Revolution** relied on the labour of children, some as young as six years old. These children worked long hours, often in horrible conditions, in factories and mines in every city and town. Child labour was one of the most serious problems that Victorian Britain faced. Social reformers called for improvements to working conditions, but they were opposed by both employers, who relied on child labour, and parents, who needed the extra income their children brought to the family.

The activities of social reformers and the evidence of parliamentary reports led to a series of **acts** of parliament which aimed to control and monitor working conditions, especially for children. The Factory Act of 1844 limited the working day for children aged between eight and thirteen to six and a half hours. The 1847 Act limited the working day for under-eighteens to ten hours. The 'Climbing Boys' Act of 1875 made it illegal to use children to climb and clean chimneys. Although these laws were often difficult to enforce, by the time Victoria died in 1901 conditions for children had greatly improved.

A woman lowers two children down a mineshaft in 1842. Children as young as five worked at least eleven hours a day in mines during Victoria's first years as queen.

These children, working in a brickyard, carry heavy lumps of wet clay from the clay heap to the brickmaker's table and back – a distance of some nineteen kilometres (twelve miles).

Factory worker describes the dangers of factory machines

An unidentified girl from Sheffield was interviewed in 1865 about her work in a knife-making factory. She describes the dangers all around the young workers as they laboured through a 14-hour working day.

I have been very careful about machines ever since a girl of nine or ten years old. We girls in some works [factories] of this kind were playing at hiding, and one about fourteen years old hid beside a drum in a wheel then not working, and it was started and crushed her to pieces. they had to pick her bones up in a basket, and that's how they buried her … girls are soft, giddy things.

A divided society

Society at the start of the nineteenth century was fairly fixed. A wealthy but small upper class earned and maintained its wealth through investments and rents from land. The middle class was made up of merchants, factory owners, professional people, such as lawyers and bankers, and small landowners. These people attributed much of their success to hard work. The largest group of people, the lower or working class, owned no land and worked mainly as farm labourers or in factories. With no paid holidays, no sick leave, no vote and unpleasant and dangerous working conditions, these people faced a difficult life, and no amount of hard work could improve their situation.

Most people – all British women and those men who did not own property – did not have the right to vote in elections. Those with power and money, who could vote, were most likely to benefit from Great Britain's increasing prosperity. The Chartist Movement, organized in 1838, tried to change this. They believed that if all men had the vote then working men would have the power to change the system. However, protests and a petition did nothing to persuade Parliament to take up their cause. Some **trade unions** tried to improve conditions, through education and self-help. Other Victorians, like Samuel Smiles, picked up on this 'self-help' message and used it as a cure for all ills. Like many wealthier Victorians, he had little understanding of the problems faced by workers who were paid a pittance for their labour or who could not find any work at all.

The 'gospel of work' and 'self-help' meant little to those Victorians whose daily life was a struggle in terrible working conditions, in which no amount of hard work would improve their lives.

Samuel Smiles writes

Samuel Smiles was a Scottish-born journalist who moved to England in his twenties. He became convinced that social improvement would come only to those who worked for it themselves. He collected his views in a popular book entitled *Self-Help* (1859). This extract comes from *Self-Help*. The language in this extract is quite difficult to understand. Smiles is saying that it is a man's duty to work hard – for his own sake and for the benefit of his country.

The career of industry which the nation has pursued, has also proved its best education. As steady application to work is the healthiest training for every individual, so is it the best discipline of a state [country]. Honourable industry travels the same road with duty; and **Providence** has closely linked both with happiness … It is true that no bread eaten by man is so sweet as that earned by his own labour, whether physical or mental. By labour the earth has been subdued, and man redeemed [saved] from barbarism; nor has a single step in civilization been made without it. Labour is not only a necessity and a duty, but a blessing: only the idler feels it to be a curse. The duty of work is written on the … muscles of the limbs, the mechanism of the hand, the nerves and lobes of the brain – the sum of whose healthy action is satisfaction and enjoyment.

The great house

The very rich formed only a small fraction of the population as a whole, and most upper-class families knew, or had heard of, each other. It was hard to break into their social circle, and there were many ways that they could tell that someone was not 'one of us'. Great formal dances, known as balls, figured largely in upper-class life. They provided entertainment and a chance to meet future husbands and wives. Whether confined to their great house in the country or spending part of their time in a London town house, the **gentry** continued with their rounds of balls, '**coming out**' and hunting.

The great house operated like a small community in itself, often employing up to a hundred servants and staff to run the house and its land and gardens. Most servants worked very long hours doing boring and dirty jobs with little in the way of reward and hardly any time off. There were rigid distinctions between the different sorts of servants, and this was reflected in their wages and some of the privileges they enjoyed.

Members of the wealthy upper class enjoying themselves during refreshment time at a **public school** cricket match. Many wealthy people had no idea how lower–class, working people lived.

Extract from survey of servants' wages

This list of servants' wages (converted into pounds and new pence) was taken from a survey of 2000 houses, conducted in England and Wales in 1891. In 1850 there were 1 million women in **domestic service**; by 1900 this number had doubled. For a comparison with modern money, a pound in 1891 would now be worth about £140.

Class of work	Age	Average annual salary
Between maid	19	£11.90
Scullery (pantry) maid	19	£13.00
Kitchen maid	20	£15.00
Nurse-housemaid	21–25	£16.00
General domestic	21–25	£14.60
Housemaid	21–25	£16.20
Nurse	25–30	£20.10
Parlour maid	25–30	£20.60
Laundry maid	25–30	£23.60
Cook	25–30	£20.20
Lady's maid	30–35	£24.70
Cook-housekeeper	40	£35.60
Housekeeper	40	£52.50

Household servants attended to almost every aspect of life as part of their job. This 1887 illustration shows a maidservant helping her mistress into her place at the dinner table.

The rising middle class

Victorian Britain saw a great surge in the number of people who could describe themselves as middle class. This middle class was made up of people who earned their living from a wide – and growing – number of jobs and professions. The middle class gained more political influence when the Reform **Act** of 1832 was passed, which gave about 250,000 men the right to vote. It also became richer, with many middle-class men making fortunes in new companies and in business generally. George Hudson, who started life as a **draper**, invested money in the railways. By 1844 he controlled more than 1600 kilometres (1000 miles) of railway line and had become one of Britain's first millionaires.

The newly rich middle classes wanted to copy the lifestyles of the landed classes. Some bought estates and built magnificent houses. They wanted servants and liked to give entertainments. To satisfy middle-class aspirations there were a number of publications giving advice on how to run houses and estates, on manners and how to bring up children.

Mrs Beeton's advice on what to wear

Isabella Beeton was an educated Victorian lady who became a popular cookery writer. Her *Book of Household Management* was published in 1861 and included 3000 recipes as well as articles on food preparation and other areas of household management. The book soon became a bible for middle-class women, who would turn to their 'Mrs Beeton's' for advice on social, business and medical matters as well as for reliable recipes. Isabella Beeton died at just 28 years of age after the birth of her fourth child. This is an extract from her *Book of Household Management*.

A lady's dress should be always suited to her circumstances, and varied for different occasions. The morning dress should be neat and simple, and suitable for the domestic duties that usually occupy the early part of the day. This dress should be changed before calling hours; but it is not in good taste to wear much jewellery except with evening dress. A lady should always aim at being well and attractively dressed whilst never allowing questions of costume to establish inordinate claims on either time or purse. In purchasing her own garments, after

A colourful advertisement for some of Mrs Beeton's books. Cooks today still refer to them for advice.

taking account of the important detail of the length of her purse, she should aim at adapting the style of the day in such a manner as best suits the requirements of her face, figure and complexion, and never allow slavish adherence to temporary fads of fashion to overrule her own sense of what is becoming and befitting. She should also bear in mind that her different costumes have to furnish her with apparel for home wear, outdoor exercise and social functions, and try to allot due relative importance to the claims of each.

Trade unions

Although Victorian Britain became the wealthiest country in the world, only a small number of people, usually businessmen or factory owners, benefited from this prosperity. The majority of those who did the actual work – the working population – had to be grateful they had a job at all. Working conditions were often dreadful and could be dangerous, but workers had little say over how much money they could earn.

At the beginning of the century it was illegal to form a **trade union** to improve workers' pay and conditions. When laws banning trade unions were **repealed** in 1824, workers began to organize and **strike** to achieve the improvements they wanted. Large trade unions, such as the Amalgamated Society of Engineers (1851), were formed to represent groups of workers involved in similar trades.

Violent disturbances in Sheffield in 1866 turned Parliament against the trade unions. The Trades Union Congress, representing a number of different unions, was formed in 1868 and pressed for the right of workers to strike peacefully. The Employers and Workmen **Act** (1875) guaranteed this right in law. From then on, workers could – and would – use the power of the strike to achieve better pay.

THE GREAT STRIKE OF DOCK LABOURERS AT THE EAST END

Ben Tillett describes how strikers raised money to support their families while not working

The London Dock Strike of 1889 showed that unions could bring a major industry to a standstill. The strike worked, and after five weeks the employers lost so much money that they gave in to the union's demands. In this passage, union leader Ben Tillett describes how the dockers raised money to support their families during the dispute.

In our marches we collected contributions in pennies [0.5p], sixpences [2.5p] and shillings [5p], from the clerks and City workers, who were touched perhaps to the point of sacrifice by the emblem of poverty and starvation carried in our procession. By these means, with the aid of the Press, money poured into our **coffers** from Trade Unions and public alike. Large sums came from abroad, especially from the British dominions [empire], whose contributions alone amounted to over £30,000. Contributions from the public sent direct by letter or collected on our marches totalled nearly £12,000; more than £1000 came in from our street box collections, and substantial amounts were obtained through the help of the Star, the Pall Mall Gazette, the Labour Elector, and other papers.

A weekly newspaper gave its readers vivid illustrations of London's 1889 Dock Strike (above left) and its organizers at their headquarters (left).

Demon drink

Excessive drinking and drunkenness have been social problems throughout European history. By the Victorian era, the problem had become especially serious among members of the industrial working class. The repetitive work at factory machines and poor living conditions drove many to drink as a way of escaping the wretchedness of their daily lives. Though factory owners knew that workers were less efficient, and could even cause accidents if they were drunk, they did little to improve the lot of their workers. Children also suffered as some workers spent their wages on alcohol, plunging their families into poverty. Crime and violence were another result of excessive drinking. Sadly some workers lost their jobs, became seriously ill or died very young because of alcohol-related diseases.

The Chartists, the **trade unions** and religious groups such as the Salvation Army (founded in 1865) insisted that 'the demon drink' lay at the heart of many social problems. They believed that **temperance** was the key to battling this problem. Their temperance meetings, held in most cities, offered people the chance to have a decent meal and to be guided towards a life without drunkenness.

The journalist James Greenwood toured some of the poorer districts of London in 1867. He recorded the words of this song, which was performed at a temperance meeting organized by a Reverend Mookow.

Come, brothers, listen unto me, and a story I'll relate,
How I in time was rescued from a wretched
    drunkard's fate.
I used to swill my nightly fill of ale, and beer, and gin,
    Nor for my wife and family cared I a single pin.
My eyes were bleared, a razed beard, likewise a
    drunkard's nose;
My children bare and naked were, because I pawned
    their clothes;
My wife I bruised, and much ill-used, and, shameful
    thing to say, **Distrained** the bed from under her
    my tavern score to pay.
But, thanks to Mr. Mookow, now all that is set aside;
Upon my wife and family I now can look with pride.
The reason's plain, I now **abstain**, and mean to, never
    fear-
I never more intend to be a slave to gin and beer.

Behind the Bar, an 1866 painting by Herbert Marshall, shows a Victorian pub scene with an assortment of drinkers, including a mother rubbing her baby's gums with whisky to calm teething pain or to send it to sleep.

Rural life

The great changes taking place in Britain during the nineteenth century were not confined to towns and cities. Despite the dramatic rise of industry, more than a quarter of the British population still worked on the land at the end of the Victorian era. For them seed drills, threshing machines and steam-powered machinery changed methods of planting and harvesting. Many of the most powerful land-owning farmers adopted a policy of enclosure, increasing the size of their farms at the expense of small farmers and land held in common for communities. Enclosure hit Scotland especially hard, and thousands of Scots were forced off their land – and often out of their country. Many of them **emigrated** to Australia, Canada or the USA.

A crowd of spectators watch a steam plough display on a farm in 1850. Steam power had a dramatic effect on farming, reducing the time it took to plough, sow and harvest crops.

During the nineteenth century the **Acts** known as the Corn Laws were **repealed**. These Acts had controlled the flow of cheaper foreign grain entering Britain, keeping prices for British farm goods high. When Ireland (an important source of grain for Britain) suffered a disastrous **famine** in the 1840s, there were more calls for allowing imports of foreign grain. Despite the repeal of the Corn Laws, British farmers still prospered between the 1850s and 1870s because the booming population needed feeding. Farm labourers, however, saw few of these benefits. Throughout the century they were forced to move from farm to farm in search of work. The Warwickshire farm workers' **strike** of 1872 was crushed, but it showed that discontent was common among farm labourers.

This folksong records the misery caused by the Highland Clearances.

The 'Highland Clearances' emptied thousands of hectares of rural Scotland of its small farmers and their families, especially in the highlands and islands.

Hush, Hush

Once our valleys were ringing
with sounds of our children singing -
but now sheep bleat o'er the evenin'
and shielings [pastures] stand empty and open.

Chorus:
Hush, hush, time to be sleepin'
hush, hush, dreams come a creepin'
dreams of peace and of freedom
so smile in your sleep, bonnie dearie.

We stood, our heads bowed in prayer
while battles laid our cottages bare -
the flames, fire, the clear mountain air
and many were dead by the morning.

Chorus

Where was our good Highland mettle?
Our men once so fearless in battle?
They stand cowered, and huddled like cattle
and wait to be shipped o'er the ocean.

Chorus

No good pleading or praying
now gone, gone, all hope of staying
hush, hush, the anchors are weighing
don't cry in your sleep, bonnie dearie.

Chorus

The Last of the Clan, **painted by Thomas Faed in 1865, shows a Highland Scot in traditional clothing leading his family away after losing his land during the Highland Clearances.**

Education

At the start of the Victorian era only the wealthy could afford to send their children to **public schools**. Vast numbers of working people were unable to read and write. Although many people felt it was important that people could read the Bible, others were worried that if working people began reading newspapers they might start calling for reform. **Trade unions** saw education as a way of releasing people from poverty. The Mechanics Institutes and special schools for adults helped teach working-class people to read and write.

All of these advances, however, were separate from each other and not part of a national plan for education. That changed with the Education **Act** of 1870, which provided that there should be a school within reach of every child. This resolve led to the building of hundreds of new schools in British villages and inner-city neighbourhoods.

Much of British education had been aimed only at boys, but girls and women began to benefit as well. The year 1872 saw the formation of the Girls' Public Day Schools Company, and Cambridge University pioneered the first two women's colleges – Girton College in 1869 and Newnham College in 1871.

Educational opportunities for women improved during Victoria's reign, although only a small number benefited. Here female students work in a laboratory at Girton College, Cambridge University in 1900.

I left school at the age of twelve … Children went to school from the age of two and a half and they had to pay school money – a penny or two pence a week. They were sent so early in order to 'get from under the feet'… If you passed an infants' school whilst lessons were on you could hear children's voices chanting C-A-T spells cat, D-O-G spells dog and so on … Many teachers were never without a cane in their hands … For good attendance one received a framed certificate. The walls of our house were covered with the things.

A group of very young school children with their teacher in 1898. Discipline and obedience were prized as highly as hard work in a Victorian classroom.

The Victorian woman

Women, even rich women, were not treated as the equals of men during Victoria's reign. A woman lost most of her property once she married. Divorces were difficult to obtain and women risked losing their children if they left their husbands. Educational opportunities were limited and there were few jobs open to poorly educated, single women apart from factory work, farming and **domestic service**. Educated women normally had to choose between writing and teaching.

Improvements did take place during Victoria's reign. The Infants Custody **Act** of 1839 gave mothers more legal rights, and the 1857 Marriage and Divorce Act gave women a better chance to divorce their husbands. A series of Married Women's Property Acts (1870, 1874, 1882, 1893) allowed women to own and inherit property and also gave them the right to enter into legal contracts and to start businesses. They did not win the right to vote in elections until 1918.

Despite the limits placed upon them, a number of women made their mark on Victorian society. Florence Nightingale made an important contribution to medical practices and the training of nurses. Dorothea Beale's tireless devotion advanced the causes of women's education and women's right to vote.

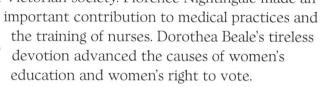

Annie Besant reports

In 1873 Annie Besant left her husband and became an **atheist**. In 1888 Besant, who was interested in the problems faced by poor working people, heard about the high dividends (share of the profits) paid to those who invested in the Bryant and May match factory, and compared these to the low wages paid to the labourers there. She wrote a series of articles that led to a public **boycott** and a **strike** of 1400, mainly women, match makers. This is an extract from one of her articles.

The hour for commencing work is 6.30 in summer and 8 in winter, work concludes at 6 p.m. ... The splendid salary of 4 shillings [20p] is subject to deductions in the shape of fines; if the feet are dirty, or the ground under the bench is left untidy, a fine of 3 pence [1.25p] is inflicted; for putting 'burnts' – matches that have caught fire during the work – on the bench 1 shilling [5p] has been forfeited, and one unhappy girl was once fined 2 shillings and 6 pence [12.5p] for some unknown crime. If a girl leaves four or five matches on her bench when she goes for a fresh 'frame' she is fined 3 pence, and in some departments a fine of 3 pence is inflicted for talking. If a girl is late she is shut out for 'half the day,' that is for the morning six hours, and 5 pence [2p] is deducted out of her day's 8 pence [3.5p]. One girl was fined 1 shilling for letting the web twist around a machine in the endeavor to save her fingers from being cut, and was sharply told to take care of the machine, 'never mind your fingers.' Another, who carried out the instructions and lost a finger thereby, was left unsupported while she was helpless. The wage covers the duty of submitting to an occasional blow from a foreman; one, who appears to be a gentleman of variable temper, 'clouts' them 'when he is mad.'

Annie Besant

Literature as a record

Much of what we know about Victorian life and values comes from the many **novels** written at that time. Great writers such as Anthony Trollope, George Eliot, Charlotte and Emily Bronte, and Charles Dickens cast an eye on life around them and drew thousands of readers into their worlds. Their novels described the life of all sorts of people – rich and poor, educated and **illiterate**, noble and evil. Many of the best-known characters in world literature – including Ebenezer Scrooge, Sherlock Holmes, Jane Eyre and Lewis Carroll's Alice – were created by Victorian authors.

The Victorian period was recorded in writing like no previous era in British history. Novels were written that described the new ideas of the time and how people reacted to them. One of the most famous authors of the period, Charles Dickens, wrote books that shocked people into thinking about the injustices that existed in Victorian society.

The works of Charles Dickens provide a vivid picture of Victorian life. In this 1843 illustration from *A Christmas Carol*, the miser Ebenezer Scrooge meets the ghost of his former partner Jacob Marley.

As more schools were teaching children to read and write, so there were more people who could enjoy this pastime. The first public libraries were opened during this era.

George Eliot writes
This passage comes from the novel *Middlemarch* (published
1871–2), written by George Eliot. Her real name was
Marian Evans, but like other women writers, she found it
easier to have her books published if it looked as if they
had been written by a man. Eliot's novel describes the life
of a small town, and the efforts made by Dorothea, who
has inherited a large estate, to improve conditions for the
local poor. In this exchange, her future brother-in-law, Sir
James Chettham, asks her about her plan to build new
cottages for farm labourers.

'Do you know, Lovegood was telling me yesterday that
you had the best notion in the world of a plan for
cottages – quite wonderful for a young lady, he
thought. You had a real "genus", to use his expression.
He said you wanted Mr Brooke to build a new set of
cottages, but he seemed to think it hardly probable
that your uncle would consent. Do you know, that is
one of the things I wish to do – I mean, on my own
estate? I should be so glad to carry out that plan of
yours, if you would let me see it. Of course, it is
sinking money; that is why people object to it.
Labourers can never pay rent to make it answer.
But, after all, it is worth doing.'

'Worth doing! yes, indeed,' said Dorothea,
energetically, forgetting her previous small **vexations**.
'I think we deserve to be beaten out of our beautiful
houses with a **scourge** of small cords – all of us who
let tenants live in such sties as we see round us. Life
in cottages might be happier than ours, if they were
real houses fit for human beings from whom we expect
duties and affections.'

39

Entertainment

At the beginning of Victoria's reign in 1837, entertainment – like so much else in Britain – was divided. The rich had a wide choice of banquets and balls, concerts and plays. Pageants and religious fetes offered amusement in country areas. Poorer people in cities, though, had little to amuse themselves in what free time they had. But, like so much else in Britain at the time, things did improve. The working week was shortened for many factory workers, giving them half of Saturday as well as Sunday to enjoy. Behind these changes were a series of new laws driven by the 'Ten Hours' movement to limit the working day. **Acts** passed in 1847 and strengthened in an 1850 act paved the way for later laws that opened up leisure time by limiting the hours of work.

Theatres and similar venues began offering entertainment for ordinary working people. The first music halls, providing songs, sketches and comedy routines, opened in 1843. Similar entertainment

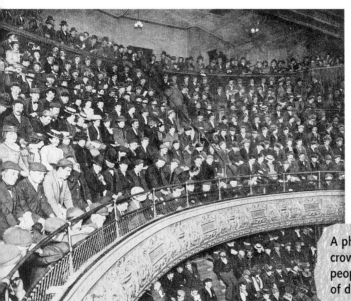

– circus acts, operettas, magic performances and pantomime – all became part of everyday life by the late nineteenth century. The increasing range of entertainment also provided new work for people – as actors, singers, stage workers and advertising people.

A photograph from 1900 shows the crowded gallery of a music hall where people would enjoy a mixed programme of drama, comic sketches and music.

Entertainment advertisement of 1879
Posters promising exciting or comical entertainment competed with each other to attract people's attention in Victorian Britain. This advertisement appeared in London in 1879.

An 1889 programme for London's Empire Theatre shows the variety of entertainment in a single evening, ranging from comic acts to ballet perfomances.

MASKELYNE & COOKE BRITAIN'S HOME OF MYSTERY EGYPTIAN HALL

Every Evening at 8. Tuesday, Thursday and Saturday at 3.
Seven years in London of unparalleled success.

A MAN'S HEAD CUT OFF WITHOUT LOSS OF LIFE

A strange statement, but no more strange than true.
In addition to the important discovery of a means of playing a brass band by mechanism, the same inventor, Mr. J. N. MASKELYNE, is showing the public, at the Egyptian Hall, London, how easy and pleasant it is to cut off Mr. Cooke's head. The clever illusion is introduced in such a manner as to provoke unrestrained laughter. No visitors to the great City should return home before witnessing Maskelyne and Cooke's Entertainment. It is one of the principal sights of London.

Private Boxes from 21s. ; Stalls, 5s. and 3s. ; Admission, 2s. and 1s.
Boxes and Stalls can be secured at any of the Agents in
the City or West End, or at the Hall.
W. Morten, Manager.

Sports and pastimes

One of the other areas of recreation that Victorians loved was sport. Working-class people, by the mid-nineteenth century, began to have some free time at weekends to take part in, or simply watch, sporting contests. A few Victorians saw sport as a way of earning extra money or – with the development of professional sports in the late nineteenth century – as a way of earning a living. Boxers had been fighting for money for more than a century, but football and rugby widened the choice of professional sports. Many of the football league teams that we know today were founded during the 1880s and 1890s.

The **public schools**, which were thriving because of all the new wealthier, middle-class students, stressed the importance of sport as a way of developing manly character. They taught sports, such as hockey, rowing and rugby. Many sports, such as rugby, badminton and lawn tennis, were invented in Victorian Britain. Others, such as football and cricket, developed the modern rules and regulations that still govern them today.

The Victorians did not simply love team sports. At home families entertained themselves with pastimes such as playing cards or reading aloud. Women and girls occupied their time with sewing and embroidery. The more adventurous pastime of cycling became popular from the 1880s onwards, and with travel made easier by the railways, families began taking trips to the seaside.

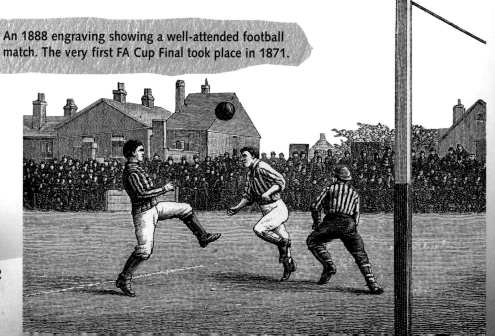

An 1888 engraving showing a well-attended football match. The very first FA Cup Final took place in 1871.

Police officer Edward Owen reports

Nineteenth-century Britain had colder winters than today, and ice-skating was a popular pastime for nearly everyone. This passage describes how people would flock to the Serpentine Lake, in London's Hyde Park, whenever the ice froze thick enough to support skaters. Policemen like Edward Owen were posted along the banks of the lake to make sure the skaters remained safe or to keep them off the ice if it began to thaw!

When the Serpentine or a portion of it is reported to be safe, all is plain sailing, and it is a fine sight to see the thousands of ladies and gentlemen, soldiers, boys and girls, all intermixed, enjoying their skating and sliding. The evenings on such occasions are novel sights, for probably there are then more people on the ice than in the daytime. The shops and other business places being closed, it becomes practically crowded. To stand on the Magazine Bridge and witness the moving mass of lights, made up of torches, **Chinese lanterns**, etc., carried by the skaters, presents a most fantastical scene. One thing I cannot understand; it seems to me to have such a fascination that some people don't care what money or property they risk in order to indulge in this recreation.

This 1900 tea advertisement shows a couple out on a cycle ride. Cycling became a popular pastime from the 1880s onwards.

Victorian art

Victorian artists responded in different ways to the changing world around them. Some tried to reflect people's sense of loss at the disappearance of the old ways of life. A group of artists known as the Pre-Raphaelites painted detailed works featuring shepherds, farmers and landscapes – without a railway line or factory chimney in sight. Photography, which was invented earlier in the century, was also used as an art form, and many of the photographs taken later in the century make valuable **primary sources** for historians studying Victorian life.

In the late 1840s and early 1850s the architects Sir Charles Barry and Augustus Pugin designed and rebuilt the Houses of Parliament in the fifteenth-century gothic style, since many Victorians believed that their own era was an echo of that 'golden age'.

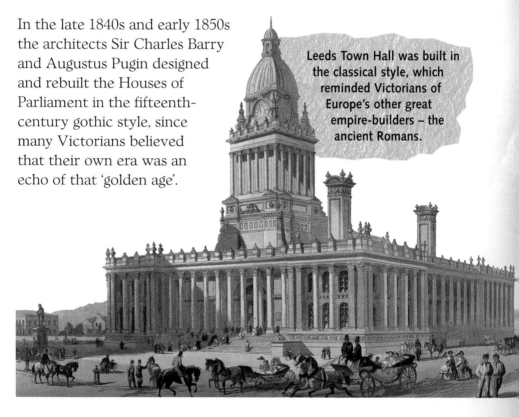

Leeds Town Hall was built in the classical style, which reminded Victorians of Europe's other great empire-builders – the ancient Romans.

Towards the end of the century artists and critics, such as William Morris and John Ruskin, claimed that mass-produced goods were destroying the livelihoods of craftsmen who had once taken a pride in their work. They also criticized many of the fussy, ornate styles in furniture and decoration that had become popular. Instead they called for styles and methods of production that depended on the imagination of the person making the goods. The works they created, though very beautiful, were too expensive for most ordinary people to buy.

Tapestry by William Morris

William Morris made this beautiful tapestry called *The Adoration of the Magi* in 1880. It was designed by the painter Sir Edward Burne-Jones and became one of Morris's most popular religious tapestries. William Morris was dedicated to reviving crafts such as weaving, stained-glass-window and furniture making. Morris wrote in an essay, 'Have nothing in your houses which you do not know to be useful or believe to be beautiful.'

William Morris was a man of many talents. He wrote poetry, painted pictures and was an excellent craftsman and businessman. Later in life he became a pioneering **socialist**.

The Golden Jubilee

Just as 1977 and 2002 were times for Jubilee celebrations in Britain, so the nineteenth century also had occasions for national pride. The Great Exhibition of 1851 was one event, Queen Victoria's Golden Jubilee, celebrating fifty years of her reign, in 1887 was another. Victoria had been proclaimed Empress of India ten years earlier and during her Golden Jubilee, India and the colonies played an important role in the state celebrations.

Overall, the economy was settled, although farming had been suffering from low prices for land and produce for more than fifteen years. Nevertheless British ships were still carrying British goods to the four corners of the world. The country felt secure, as British troops had not been involved in a major European war for more than thirty years, although they had been fighting in other areas of the world, especially in India and Africa.

The national mood in 1887 was confident and enthusiastic, and the celebrations reflected this. Special events in London, attended by Victoria herself, took place throughout the year, and the atmosphere outside the capital city was also jubilant. Towns and villages organized special events – reaching a peak on 22 June 1887, the date set aside for the celebrations.

Thousands of Londoners lined the streets to cheer Queen Victoria during her Jubilee procession in June 1887.

On the 21st of June, which marked the completion of the mystic
period of fifty years and a day in the reign of Queen Victoria,
the village street was decorated with festoons of greenery from
side to side, and a peal was rung before the daily ten o'clock
service, to which a special service hymn and prayer were added.

At 3 p.m. the Village Church of Britain Temperance Society
Fife and Drum Band, reinforced from Ixworth and Thurston,
paraded the street from end to end and back again, and then up
to the Church door. The choir then proceeded up the church
singing the hymn

'King of kings Thy blessing shed
On our anointed Sovereign's head'

The elders amused themselves in the Vicarage gardens, and in
the portion of Mr Green's park set apart for the sports till these
began. They lasted till dark, and, indeed some had to be
curtailed owing to want of light.

Then came the fireworks, which were many and excellent, and
did not conclude till past eleven o'clock at night. They ended
with an external illumination of the church by means of
changing coloured lights, which served to guide the spectators
towards their homes, while the village street was prettily
decorated with **Chinese lanterns**.

Christian duty

Far more people attended church in Victorian Britain than they do today. Jews, Muslims and people of other faiths were free to practise their own religions. However, most British people were Christian. Many people believed that the Bible was the direct word of God, with strict commandments about how people should behave. One of the most important commandments for the Victorians was 'to keep holy the Sabbath (Sunday)', which was intended as a day of rest and worship. Many people, especially from the middle class, went to church or chapel two or even three times on a Sunday. Shops and places of entertainment remained closed.

Belief in God went far beyond observing Sundays, however. Many Christian groups, such as the Methodists, Quakers and Salvation Army, believed that all Christians had a duty to help improve the lives of others. William Booth, who founded the Salvation Army in 1865, wanted to help those people who did not go to church. He also campaigned against the drinking of alcohol. Booth's army, with its military style uniforms and its brass bands, soon spread around the world.

The Salvation Army was founded as a religious organization that aimed to improve living conditions in Britain and beyond. This chart from 1890 shows how the organization thought they could solve people's problems.

David Livingstone's speech

Other Christians, called **missionaries**, travelled abroad believing it was their duty to teach the Christian religion to those who had not heard about it. David Livingstone, the Scottish missionary and explorer, travelled across much of Africa between 1840 and 1873, spreading Christianity and recording the geography and customs of the African peoples. This extract comes from a speech he gave at Cambridge University in 1857.

My object in going into the country south of the desert was to instruct the natives in a knowledge of Christianity, but many circumstances prevented my living amongst them more than seven years, amongst which were considerations arising out of the slave system carried on by the Dutch Boers. I resolved to go into the country beyond, and soon found that, for the purposes of commerce, it was necessary to have a path to the sea. I might have gone on instructing the natives in religion, but as civilization and Christianity must go on together, I was obliged to find a path to the sea, in order that I should not sink to the level of the natives. The chief was overjoyed at the suggestion, and furnished me with twenty-seven men, and canoes, and provisions, and presents for the tribes through whose country we had to pass.

What have we learnt from the Victorians?

In looking through the **primary sources** in this book, we can see the range of opinion and outlook that marked Victorian society. There is plenty of evidence of the terrible living and working conditions that people suffered. At the same time we can hear the voices of those who worked hard to change those conditions, as on pages 13 and 37. It is their belief in progress which chiefly distinguishes the Victorians from people of other ages, though of course some Victorians did not want to see change at all. Generally, however, most were pleased with their achievements, their literature, their scientific discoveries and inventions, their missionary and charitable efforts; but they also thought that they could do better, and that subsequent generations would do better still. They took it for granted that there would be 'progress'.

In nearly every aspect of daily life, from medicine, science and transport, to entertainment, we reap the benefits of the progress that the Victorians made. We also face many of the same conflicts that they did: industrial disputes, debates about education and health, science versus religion and so on. Only time will tell if we are any better or worse at solving these problems than the Victorians.

A newspaper journalist reflects on the end of an era
The following extract appeared in *The Times* on 23 January 1901, the day after Queen Victoria died. The writer is worried about the state of Britain at the end of an era. In fact, as the writer suggests, 'others', probably meaning the USA and Germany, were catching up with Britain in terms of industrial growth and trade. Britain's position as the wealthiest country in the world was under threat.

The Times

23 January 1901

At the close of the reign we are finding ourselves somewhat less secure of our position than we could desire, and somewhat less abreast of the problems of the age than we ought to be, considering the initial advantages we secured … Others have learned our lessons and bettered our instructions while we have been too easily content to rely upon the methods which were effective a generation or two ago. In this way is the Victorian age defined at its end as well as at its beginning.

The end of an era. Mourners watch the gun carriage carrying Queen Victoria's coffin making its stately way through London during her funeral in 1901.

Timeline

1815	Corn Laws enacted to prevent entry of cheap grain and keep farm wages low and bread prices high.
1819	Birth of Victoria.
1820	Death of King George III. The Prince Regent becomes George IV.
1830	Death of George IV. William IV becomes king.
1837	William IV dies and Victoria becomes queen.
1840	Victoria marries Albert of Saxe-Coburg-Gotha, who becomes known as the Prince Consort.
	The Penny Post is established.
1842	The Mines **Act** bans employment of boys younger than ten and all girls and women from working in underground mines.
1843	Charles Dickens writes *A Christmas Carol*. Music halls and Christmas cards begin to appear.
1846	Corn Laws **repealed**.
	First operation in Britain performed under **anaesthesia**.
1847	Potato **famine** in Ireland; millions either starve or **emigrate** to Great Britain, Australia and the USA.
	Britain's new Ten Hours Bill limits the working day to ten hours.
1848	First Public Health Act passed.
1851	The Great Exhibition opens in London in the Crystal Palace.
1854	Great Britain enters the Crimean War which started in 1853. Great Britain, France and Turkey fight against Russia; Florence Nightingale achieves fame there and founds the nursing profession.
1857	Transatlantic telegraph cable laid between Britain and the USA.
1859	Charles Darwin publishes *On the Origin of Species*.
1861	Prince Albert dies; Victoria mourns until her death in 1901.
1865	The Salvation Army founded.
1869	First bicycle factory established.
1867	The Reform Bill extends voting rights to most working-class men.
1870	The Education Act provides free education for all children up to the age of eleven.
1875	The Employers and Workmen Act guarantees the right of **trade unions** to call **strikes**.
	Public Health Act passed.
1877	Victoria crowned Empress of India; the British Empire is at its peak.
1887	Victoria's Golden Jubilee celebrated.
1889	The Great Dock Strike ends with the first major trade-union victory.
1901	Victoria dies.

Find out more

Books & websites

Life and World of Queen Victoria, Brian Williams, (Heinemann Library, 2002)
People in the Past, Victorian Children, Brenda Williams, (Heinemann Library, 2003)
The Victorians in Britain, Peter Chrisp, (Franklin Watts, 1999)
Turning Points: The Steam Engine, Richard Tames, (Heinemann Library, 2000)
Victorian Village Life, Neil Philip, (Idbury, Village Press), 1993

Go Exploring! Log on to Heinemann's online history resource.
www.heinemannexplore.co.uk

www.historyteacher.net/APEuroCourse/APEuro_Main_Weblinks_Page.html
This site has a variety of primary sources and also has several sound files for
downloading.

www.spartacus.schoolnet.co.uk
The Spartacus site contains a wealth of information about many aspects of Victorian
Britain, with a useful search engine for finding specific information.

www.victorianlondon.org
This site has a wide variety of documents and informative articles about life in
nineteenth-century London.

www.victorianstation.com
This site is devoted to Victorian Britain, with special emphasis on Queen Victoria
herself. There is a fascinating section on quotes by Victoria, recorded throughout
her reign.

List of primary sources

The author and publisher gratefully acknowledge the following publications and websites from which written sources in the book are drawn. In some cases the wording or sentence structure has been simplified to make the material more appropriate for a school readership.

P.9 *The Aylesbury News: News from the English Countryside 1750–1850*, Clifford Morsley, (Harrap, 1979)

P.11 http://members.tripod.com/~midgley/rowlandhill.html from extract from *The Life of Sir Rowland Hill and the Penny Postage*, R. and G. Birkbeck Hill, 1880

P.13 Hector Gavin: www.victorianlondon.org/index1.htm

P.15 Charles Dickens: www.victorianlondon.org/index1.htm

P.17 Charles Darwin: quoted in *For Country and Queen: Britain in the Victorian Age*, Margaret Drabble, (Andre Deutsch, 1978)

P.19 *Art Journal* http://www.speel.demon.co.uk/other/grtexhib.htm
The *Sun* www.channel4.com/learning/main/netnotes/dsp_series.cfm?sectionid=349

P.21 quoted in *For Country and Queen: Britain in the Victorian Age*, Margaret Drabble, (Andre Deutsch, 1978)

P.23 Samuel Smiles:
edweb.tusd.k12.az.us/UHS/WebSite/courses/WC/Historiography/industrialization_and _social.htm

P.25 http://learningcurve.pro.gov.uk/victorianbritain/divided/default.htm

P.27 Isabella Beeton: www.fandom.net/~daeron/Beeton/beeton1.html.

P.29 Ben Tillett: www.spartacus.schoolnet.co.uk/TUdockers.html

P.31 James Greenwood: www.victorianlondon.org/index1.htm

P.33 http://site.yahoo.net/np/versesong.html

P.35 'Old People's Reminiscences', Lancashire Record Office, DDX.9783/3/13

P.37 Annie Besant: 'White Slavery in London' reprinted on:
http://www.wwnorton.com/nael/nto/victorian/industrial/besantfrm.htm

P.39 George Eliot, *Middlemarch*, (Penguin Classics, 1994 p.31)

P.41 www.victorianlondon.org/

P.43 Edward Owen:www.victorianlondon.org/

P.45 *The Adoration of the Magi* tapestry made by William Morris and Co. 1890

P.47 Reverend C.W. Jones:www.pakenham-village.co.uk/History/PakRJ1887.htm

P.49 David Livingstone: http://www.cooper.edu/humanities/classes/coreclasses/ hss3/d_livingstone.html

P.51 *The Victorian Scene: 1837–1901*, by Nicolas Bentley, (Weidenfeld & Nicolson, 1968)

Glossary

abstain   hold back from doing something

act   (of parliament) law passed by parliament

anaesthesia   deadening of pain, usually caused by drugs, so the patient doesn't feel pain during an operation

antiseptic   substance that stops the spread of germs

atheist   someone who does not believe in the existence of God

bias   judgement that is based on personal opinion

boycott   refuse to use or have anything to do with something, usually as a form of protest

Chinese lantern   collapsible lantern made of thin paper, often used as a decoration

cholera   disease, often fatal, which causes acute stomach pain, vomiting and diarrhoea and which can easily be passed on to others

coffers   funds held in reserve for a group or institution

colony   group of people separated from, but governed by, another country

coming out   event, usually a ball, where wealthy young women first join adults at social occasions

distrain   seize property from someone until that person can repay a debt

domestic service   working as a servant in wealthier people's houses

draper   someone who sells cloth

emigrate   leave one country and settle in another

epidemic   widespread outbreak of disease that spreads quickly

evolution   change in a type of plant or animal over generations, suggesting that the strongest in one generation are likelier to reproduce and pass on their characteristics to later generations

famine   terrible, and often prolonged, shortage of food

festoon   string or chain of flowers or ribbons, hanging in a curve as a decoration

gentry   class of people in Britain below the nobility, but still owning large amounts of land and other property

gibbet   wooden frame on which convicted criminals were hanged

hygiene   attention to cleanliness and the avoidance of spreading germs

illiterate   unable to read or write

Industrial Revolution   period, beginning in Britain in the 1700s, during which new inventions and methods of working brought about rapid changes in industry

manufacture   making a large number of goods using machines

missionary   person sent to another country specially to spread the Christian religion

naturalist   scientist who studies the natural world

novel   work of literature, usually much longer than a short story, in which invented characters are involved in a series of events

primary source   original account or image describing a historical event or era

Providence   the protective care of God

public school   school that charges fees. Typically only children of the wealthy would attend such schools.

repeal   annul or overturn an act of law

Royal Commission   organization given royal approval to suggest government action

scourge   whip or lash used to punish people

secondary source   historical account recorded some time after the events and by someone who was not there at the time

socialist   someone who believes wealth should be shared equally and that the main industries should be controlled by the government

species   specific category of plant or animal; members of the same species share many similar characteristics

strike   stop work until some improvement to working conditions is made; usually done by a group of workers in the same type of work or employed at the same business

temperance   deliberate choice not to drink alcohol

trade union   organization of workers, usually in the same type of trade or work, which aims to improve the working conditions of its members

transported   sent by force to another country as a punishment. Criminals were often transported to Australia and were forced to stay there for a long time, even for minor offences.

tuberculosis   infectious disease that leads to small swellings in many parts of the body, especially the lungs

turbine   type of engine

typhus   infectious disease, transmitted by lice and fleas and causing fatigue, violent headaches and reddish spots on the body

vexation   something that annoys or is a nuisance

workhouse   institution for the very poor where they would receive food and shelter in return for work

Index